Episcopacy.

EPISCOPACY:

AN

ABRIDGMENT OF PART OF A DISSERTATION

UPON

"THE CHRISTIAN MINISTRY."

BY

REV. J. B. LIGHTFOOT, D.D.,

HULSEAN PROFESSOR OF DIVINITY IN CAMBRIDGE UNIVERSITY, ENGLAND

PUBLISHED BY

THE LATIMER ASSOCIATION.

NEW-YORK.

1872.

Copies of this Tract are to be had from A. D. F. RANDOLPH & CO., 770 Broadway, New-York. Price, ten cents per copy.

INTRODUCTORY.

This tract, issued under the auspices of the Latimer Association, a society composed of clergymen of the Protestant Episcopal Church, is an abridgment of that part of the dissertation on the Christian Ministry, by Dr. Lightfoot, which refers to the constitution and history of that ministry. The other point of the treatise, whether it is, or is not, sacerdotal in its nature, is not here adverted to, but is left for separate treatment.

This abridgment is made in order to lay before the clergy and laity, in a brief form, for their study, the argument upon a great question of the day that is contained in an essay which is rather long and intended for students, as well as still unpublished in this country. It is to be found in the volume that contains the commentary on the Epistle to the Philippians by the same author, and reference can be made thereto for verification of statements and of quotations herein made.

The author, Rev. J. B. Lightfoot, D.D., is Hulsean Professor of Divinity in Trinity College, Cambridge, England, and one of the most eminent of the scholars that adorn the Anglican Church, ranking with Ellicott, Wordsworth, and Alford. He has written commentaries on the Epistles to the Galatians and the Philippians, as also on the two uncanonical Epistles of Clement of Rome to the Corinthians. These show him to be an author whose statements are to be respected and whose learning and critical power make his arguments too weighty to be refuted by mere appeal to church tradition, or to the authority of great but uncritical writers.

As evidence of how the author is esteemed in England, the following is the opinion entertained of him by the well-known Bishop of Ely, Harold Browne, who calls him, "one of the ablest, most learned, and most candid of living divines." (Sermon on "The Parish Deaconess." *Note.*)

They who desire to prosecute the matter still further, and ascertain more regarding the latest researches, made in a calm and scholarly manner, as to what the Word of God teaches concerning the Christian ministry, are referred to that exceedingly valuable work, recently issued, *The Ecclesiastical Polity of the New Testament*, by Rev. G. A. Jacob, D.D., of London.

EPISCOPACY.

I.

THE MINISTRY, AS SET FORTH IN THE NEW TESTAMENT.

THE Christian ideal is a holy season, extending the whole year round, a temple confined only by the limits of the habitable world, and a priesthood coextensive with the human race. But loyalty to this ideal is not incompatible with organization. As the church grew, it became necessary, from the nature of the case, to have rules and officers. The celebration of the first day in the week, and annual festivals established afterward, were found valuable to stimulate and direct devotion. Particular edifices were required for worship. Yet the Apostles always taught that these were means, not ends. They proclaimed that "God dwelleth not in temples made with hands," and denounced those who "observed days and months and seasons and years," thereby meaning to reprove the false idea of giving to mere expedients and conveniences an intrinsic value. These institutions were accessories, not essential parts of the Gospel of God to man. Consequently, they must never obscure true Christian worship nor restrict Christian liberty.

It was so with the ministry. It became necessary to have special officers for the administration of the many duties, such as teaching, ruling, alms-giving, etc. But they are not the *essence* of the Christian religion. Were the clergy *priests*, then they would be an integral part of the Gospel, the means of communicating its blessings. But all believers are priests, and are themselves entitled to immediate access to God, through Christ, as well as bound to tell of Jesus to others; therefore, the ministry is not essential to the being of the church of Christ; it is only required for its proper and well-ordered administration.

In the statements bearing on the constitution of the church, in the New Testament, we find two kinds of ministries.

The one was distinguished by certain special functions and miraculous "powers," or "gifts." There is a setting forth of the nature of this ministry in 1 Cor. 12. But its character showed it was only temporary. The powers conferred upon those whom the Holy Spirit called to it, such as healing, speaking with tongues, inspired expositions and appeals, or "prophesyings," were such as were peculiarly required at the establishment of the church. Consequently, it passed away, its "gifts" ceased, when God deemed its work done, and the only analogue to it now is the ministry that every Christian does for Christ, or should do, according to his opportunities.

But we also find traces of another kind of ministry, one established to govern and instruct the church. It is spoken of with frequency, and we find the terms "elders," "deacons," "pastors," and others, used, describing it as one that was more settled and regulated than that of gifts. This, from its nature, as intended to govern and teach, was to be permanent. It was not only adapted to the infancy of the church, but was to be always needed.

At first, the temporary ministry was, therefore, the more prominent; but as the Chistian communities became larger and more ordered, the other emerged from a subordinate place, and, while the former fell away, the latter grew in importance, ultimately surviving alone, as it has unto this day.

Now, as our inquiry is regarding this permanent ministry, what is taught concerning it in the Scriptures?

The Acts of the Apostles show that, at first, the Apostles were the sole directors of the church, the only officers, in all its relations. But the growth of the church, and the many kinds of new duties required, called for aid. To relieve themselves, they delivered into the hands of other selected officers the simpler and inferior functions of the many which they had previously discharged alone.

First, they established the diaconate. They appointed *deacons.* Complaints came to their ears that the Hellenist (Jews from Greek, and other Greek-speaking, regions) widows had been neglected in the distribution of food and alms in the church, that was so far confined to Jerusalem. To remedy this, the Apostles told the people to choose seven men, proper to attend to that class of duties, and they would ordain them. This took place, (Acts 6,) and the office thus instituted was maintained thereafter. For, though these seven are never called "deacons," yet the facts that their work is spoken of by a word that means to do the work of a deacon, that their duties were the same as those of others who were called by that title, and that tradition is full and unanimous on the subject, lead to a belief that with them this office began. It spread from Jerusalem throughout the whole church, as we find from the epistles. The duties of the diaconate were, primarily, those connected with the relief of the poor. But they had many opportunities in their labors to do far more, even to preach, and Philip and Stephen showed how they could use these occasions. Several passages, such as 1 Tim. 3 : 8, etc., show that teaching was not essentially a part of the office.

We also find in the New Testament a class of officers called "presbyters," (of which Greek term the word "elder" is only a translation,) or "bishops," likewise translated sometimes into "overseers."

Nothing, however, is told us concerning their first appointment, or when the office arose. The earliest mention of them is in Acts 11 : 30, where they are spoken of as a recognized, well-known order in the church at Jerusalem, to whom money was sent which had been contributed for the Christians there suffering from famine.

How can we account for this absence of any record of the institution of the presbyterate? The probable reason was that it was not a new, special creation, but one that arose without any direct or required intervention of the Apostles, and in this way: The Jews worshipped, not only as required in the Temple, but also in synagogues. Furthermore, each sect, or school, had its own synagogues. Even the fact that Jews in Jerusalem, or elsewhere, had come from the same lands, whither their ancestors had been exiled, was a ground for forming separate congregations, such as those of the Cyrenians and Alexandrians, and others which are spoken of in the New Testament. These synagogues were always formed on one model, that is, governed by selected officers, called "elders," (old men,) or "presbyters." Now, the

Christians in Jerusalem, and elsewhere, did not, at first, withdraw from all Judaism and cut loose from their nation or faith; they simply formed synagogues by themselves, and were regarded, and tolerated more or less, as a sect, with its own congregations and places of worship, just as the Essenes or the Libertines were. When they came to form these synagogues, they organized them, like all others about them, with elders or presbyters to rule them, undoubtedly with Apostolic sanction, and so this order of ministers in the church originated. The order was extended, as we learn from the Acts and Epistles, by the Apostles, to those Gentile churches where the Christians, not being Jews, would not have had such a model as the synagogue to copy.

But, as soon as the presbyterate is spoken of, it is found to be the ruling body in Jerusalem, which church was, of course, the most prominent then. They receive and distribute alms. They share, with the Twelve, the calling, debating, and the decreeing of the council mentioned in Acts 15, and they receive Paul on his last visit.

But how did the presbyters come to be called "bishops" or "episcopoi," which is the Greek word, from which the other is derived?

That *bishop* and *presbyter* mean the same office is clear, because the names are interchanged in such cases as Phil. 1 : 1; Acts 20 : 28; Titus 1 : 7, etc. No one denies this, however, now. The solution seems to be found in the fact that presbyters of the Gentile churches, and only of these, are called by the former name. This title was confined to them, and the other was given to *Jewish Christian* ministers. The officer who would be called, by the latter, a presbyter, because that was the name given to analogous officers in the ancient faith, would be called "overseer" or "episcopos" by the Gentiles, (who spoke Greek,) because that was to them a proper name for one with such duties. It is also thought that the name was given, because they were used to hearing clubs or confraternities call their ruling officers by that title.

So do we find that, under the Apostles, the orders of deacon and presbyter were clearly instituted. Is there any trace of that third and higher rank which has since existed, called especially *bishops*, or *the episcopate?* Let us answer this.

At an early date, the idea was advanced by Theodoret, which is still held by many, that the episcopate was the continuation of the apostolate, and meant officers of the same rank, that succeeded them under another name, and that, for this reason, no special mention is made of the origin of the former. But there militates against this, the simple, obvious fact that the functions were different, and are so still. The apostolate was a peculiar office, adapted to the founding of the church, and in nowise resembled the episcopate. It ceased to be, when its work was done. Theodoret gives, as his authority for his theory, the fact that, while in the opening of the Epistle to the Galatians, presbyters and deacons are addressed, in chap. 2, v. 25, Epaphroditus is (in the Greek) termed an "apostle," which proves, says he, the continuation of the apostolate beyond the Twelve. But the passage shows that Epaphroditus was only the apostle, or messenger, sent by that church to Paul with alms, not so called as an officer thereof.

The *name* suggests the origin of the episcopate. The term "bishop" was at first applied to all presbyters, but was afterward restricted to a higher rank of ministers. This seems to indicate that the order of bishops rose upward, out of the presbyterate, was not developed downward, out of the apostolate; that it came, not from localizing apostles, with lessened powers, but from elevating some presbyters above others and giving them *par excellence* the name of "overseers" or "bishops." It is difficult to see how any other pedigree for the episcopate can be harmonized with this fact regarding the name.

If this is so, we would expect to find in Jerusalem, the first and oldest of the churches, the earliest instance of this developed form of the ministry, or of an approach to it, and we are not disappointed. James, the Lord's brother, within apostolic times, can alone be regarded as holding any thing like the position of a bishop, in the later sense of the term. In St. Paul's language, he takes a precedence even of Peter and John, when the affairs of the Jewish church are in question. (Gal. 2 : 9.) In the Acts, he appears as the local representative of that church in Jerusalem; he presides at the council, suggests and frames the decree, receives Apostles, and is deferred to, generally, though he was not of the Twelve. Yet, though prominent, he appears as a member of a body. Peter desires that his deliverance be reported to "James and the brethren." When Paul visits him, all the presbyters are present. Sometimes he is mentioned alone; at other times he is omitted and the body of presbyters mentioned. From this it may be inferred that he was a member of the presbytery, yet holding a superior position—the president of the college. How he reached it is not told us, nor is the character of his powers and duties.

But, while there seems to be such an organization of the church in the Holy City, there is no trace of any thing like it among Gentile Christians, in the New Testament. As regards them, there are two stages of development perceptible :

At first, the Apostles exercised all the care of these churches themselves, either by visits or by messages. Such were St. Paul's relations to that of Corinth.

Thereafter, when Christianity was more widely spread, they could not so attend to all the duties, and delegated disciples to dwell, for a longer or shorter time, in certain places and direct affairs. The pastoral epistles represent this stage. Timothy and Titus were not, as has been claimed, in later ages, only, settled bishops of Ephesus and Crete, but had temporary commissions, whose approaching close is indicated in various places. (See 1 Tim. 1 : 3 ; 3 : 14 ; 2 Tim. 4 : 9, 21 ; Titus 1 : 5 ; 3 : 12.)

The Scriptures do not carry us further than this, regarding the organization of the church. Some claim that the "Angels" of the churches, mentioned in the Revelation of St. John, were bishops ; but it is a very doubtful, if not untenable, position. The language of the context is all symbolical. Whoever the Angel was, he is held responsible for the church to an extent that is unsuited to any human officer, and things are said of him that can not be literally predicated of men. That the Angel of Thyatira is reproved for being led astray by his "wife Jezebel," shows that the usual literal interpretation that he was a bishop, is erroneous. Furthermore, the Angels are represented by "stars" and the churches by "candlesticks ;" that is, the bishops are as much greater than the churches (if they are bishops) as stars are than candles, which is not to be admitted. The "Angels" seem to be real angels, in some way not explained to us, representing the churches. (With this view Alford coincides, who quotes, as agreeing with him, Origen, Gregory Nazianzen, and Ambrose.) And, if they were bishops, then, within two or three years of the writing of Epistles, wherein there is no trace of episcopacy, it is found fully developed in Asia Minor, which is too short a time for such an important change to have taken place. Therefore, at the close of the New Testament canon, about A.D. 70, there is no trace of any episcopate in the church, except that solitary case of James at Jerusalem, where the character of the man and his relation to the Lord would secure that prominence among his presbyterial peers, analogous to an episcopal rank, which, as we infer from the above quotations, was held by him.

II.

THE GOVERNMENT OF THE CHURCH AFTER THE CLOSE OF INSPIRATION.

Although there was no episcopate founded by the year 70, yet it can not be denied that, shortly after A.D. 100, it was firmly established, and that before A.D. 200 it was, so far as we know, universally received.

How did the office arise so soon after the last canonical book was written? Rothe, in his famous treatise, advances a theory, which is this: Errors of all kinds were rife and distracting the church. Paul, Peter, James, and others were dead. Jerusalem had fallen, and the centre, the keystone, was thus removed. Disintegration seemed impending and organization was demanded.

Then there were probably surviving John, Philip, and Andrew, and others still of the Twelve, who took in hand this task of organization. They saw how an overseership of a prominent presbyter had been adorned and blessed in Jerusalem, and made it the model by which they labored, thus recommending the adoption of an office that would, and did, act as a bond of union among the churches. Rothe gives quotations from old authors in support of this, that, however, do not bear the weight he puts upon them; for he shows too great readiness to twist them in his own behalf, in order to prove that a *council was held* of the surviving Apostles, after the fall of Jerusalem, when the plan was devised.

Yet this view is undoubtedly based on truth. The

state of the church demanded certainly some such organization, and the precedent of the mother church in Jerusalem, if it was so governed, as we have inferred, was one that met the case and that would be naturally followed. Furthermore, episcopacy is first found complete in Asia Minor, where St. John, at any rate, lived until nearly A.D. 100, and it is presumable his advice and sanction were sought. The presbyters in each church had formed a council or college. There must have been a presiding officer, and who so well adapted as he for selection to represent that church in its relations to others? What more natural than that to him should be delegated the executive powers that were constantly calling for exercise?

In this way would episcopacy seem to have arisen in the years closely following the close of the canon, and its value to the church, as well as the presumed sanction of the eminent apostle, in whose life-time it originated, led to its gradual adoption throughout Christendom.

Let us now, by a review of the early history of the principal churches in this regard, notice whether facts confirm this theory and show that the office was generally accepted by Christians in all lands before A.D. 200.

1. As to Jerusalem, various historians give the names of Symeon and others, as successors of St. James in the office; but many question the value of the list. Yet there is no doubt that, in A.D. 130, Marcus was truly bishop there.

As to other parts of Palestine, we have no clear evidence of an episcopate, until about A.D. 190, when bishops of three cities are found signing an important letter regarding the date of Easter. Yet it is difficult to believe that statements are all false, which make the office universal at a much earlier date, and we should expect it would be soon copied from the example of the Holy City.

2. Of the church at Antioch, we have early records. Ignatius, the second, traditionally, in the succession after Peter, was undoubtedly bishop of that city, since he thus speaks of himself and is so spoken of by others. He also urges on his correspondents the duty of obedience to their bishops, and from his time the list is complete of those who ruled the metropolis of Gentile Christendom.

3. Of the early history of the Syrian church, we have no trustworthy record.

4. In Asia Minor, we have clear traces of episcopacy at an early date. About A.D. 110, Ignatius calls Onesimus bishop of Ephesus, and Polycarp, of Smyrna. This, and other evidence of Irenæus and Polycrates can not be reasonably questioned. Equally unequivocal is the evidence as to bishops at that time in Hierapolis, Laodicea, Sardis, Sinope, Amastris, Magnesia, and Tralles. In fact, if historical documents are worth any thing, episcopacy can be shown to have prevailed throughout Asia Minor early in the second century, while, by A.D. 175, synods were already held, and we have many letters written by bishops by that time, of whom Polycrates says "crowds" met to consider the date of Easter.

5. In Macedonia and Greece, the evidence is faint. In Philippi, there was no bishop in A.D. 110, for Polycarp writes to the church such a letter as he could not, had there been any; refers to none, speaks as if there were none. So in Corinth; Clement wrote to that church about A.D. 95, but his letter is such that it excludes the possibility of its having a bishop; yet it had one fifty

years later. As to Athens, a letter of one Dionysius first speaks of the church there, and shows it had a bishop at the beginning of the second century, or about A.D. 110.

6. In Crete, this same letter of Dionysius shows it had an episcopate at the same era.

7. We know nothing of the Thracian church until about A.D. 190, when there is mentioned the bishop of Debeltum, a small city. Yet this very fact shows the institution to be widely spread and not very recent.

8. We turn to Rome and find evidence hopelessly conflicting and scanty. About A.D. 95, Clement writes *from* Rome to Corinth, yet he does not mention himself as distinct from the church; he speaks of the divinely instituted ministry, yet does not refer to any episcopate; he uses the word "bishop" as synonymous with "presbyter." On his way to martyrdom, (A.D. 115,) Ignatius writes *to* the Romans, yet makes no reference to any bishop there; while, in his other extant letters, he strongly advocates episcopacy. Again, "The Shepherd of Hermas," written several years later, speaks of the church at Rome in such a way that we can not decide from it if there was a bishop there or not.

On the other hand, Hegesippus, about A.D. 150, says he drew up a list of the bishops of Rome to that time, and Irenæus did the same. But the lists preserved are irreconcilably discordant. We can only feel sure that Linus, in A.D. 68, and Anacletus, in A.D. 80, were prominent in the church, and that Clement, in A.D. 92, held a position like the bishopric. This last was, however, not such as bishops became, for Ignatius and Hermas do not allude to him in addressing the church; yet he was its foremost presbyter, beyond a doubt. The Roman episcopate is not clear and historical until Pius, in A.D.

142, when controversy brought that church into the prominence it has maintained ever since.

9. In Gaul, we have no historical records of the church before Pothinus, Bishop of Lyons, who was martyred A.D. 177.

10. Of the African church, we know nothing until the close of the second century. But the number of bishops at early synods would seem to show an early and rapid spread of the office.

11. The church at Alexandria was probably founded in apostolic times. In A.D. 134, we have a reference to it, which speaks of its bishop, in a letter of the Emperor Hadrian. At the close of that century, Clement of Alexandria writes of the ministry and sometimes speaks of *two orders*, deacons and presbyters, sometimes of a *third.* This shows that, about A.D. 200, the bishop of this great city was regarded as not so distinct from the presbytery as to be separate from them.

These references evidence an early and extensive adoption of the episcopate in the church, and some writers, between A.D. 150 and A.D. 200, speak as if they had never known any other form of church government.

And these notices also throw light on the origin of the office. They show, first, that the episcopate rose out of the presbyterate, and was not the apostolate continued; second, that it did not spread at a uniform rate in all parts, but was a progressive development; third, the fact that it rose and spread soonest in Asia Minor, can not be dissociated from the influence of John and of the other Apostles who may have lived nearly to the end of the first century.

III.

THE RELATION OF THE BISHOP TO THE PRESBYTERY.

As we have seen, Clement at Rome, the Bishop of Alexandria, and others, if bishops, were not yet regarded as a separate order of men from the presbytery. But later than this, the evidence is abundant that they were all viewed as *chief presbyters*, called bishops, not as a third, independent order or class.

Irenæus, Bishop of Lyons, died A.D. 202, is very clear in his setting forth of this idea. He speaks of bishops repeatedly as "presbyters," who occupy "the chief seat." Language which refers manifestly to the episcopal office, yet urges obedience to "presbyters." Were it needed, quotations could be multiplied.

Clement of Alexandria, writing A.D. 194, defines this idea still more clearly. He divides the ministry into presbyters and deacons, including bishops, and their duties, in the former class. Ambrosiaster, one hundred and fifty years later, is as explicit. He says there is *one ordination of bishop and presbyter, for they are the same*, but "he is a bishop who is first among the presbyters." St. Jerome, died 420, dwells at length on the theme. He says three times that "presbyters are the same as bishops," and refers to the Epistle to the Philippians as proof. He adds also, "But gradually all the responsibility was referred to a single person—therefore, as presbyters know that, *by the custom of the church*, they are subject to him who shall have been set over them, so let bishops know that they are superior to presbyters, *more owing to custom than to any actual ordinance of the Lord,*" etc. And Augustine, the great father, says to Jerome, "Although, *according to titles of honor, which the practice of the church has made valid,* the episcopate is greater than the presbytery, yet in many things Augustine is less than Jerome."

These are great names, and they all show that, long after the apostolic days, it was not claimed that a bishop was of a different order from a presbyter, as a deacon is, but all held him to be only a chief, ruling presbyter. In fact, this was never claimed until the era of the Reformation.

Furthermore, it seems to be substantiated that, until A.D. 313, in Alexandria, the presbyters chose and ordained their bishops. The evidence is hard to refute, and gains confirmation from the fact that until A.D. 190, there was no other bishop in Egypt, so that the ordination had to be done by the clergy, who would naturally continue the custom beyond that time, as long as possible.

In A.D. 314, a council, held at Ancyra, decreed that country bishops should not ordain presbyters and deacons, *nor even should it be allowed to* "*city presbyters,* except permission be given to each parish by the bishop in writing."

These two cases also show that bishops were not regarded as a separate order, but a higher class of presbyters, who might also ordain, as well as they. Yet, unquestionably, this right of ordination was at first generally, and soon universally, reserved to bishops.

IV.

DEVELOPMENT OF THE PREROGATIVES OF THE EPISCOPATE.

It is clear from what has been said that the earliest bishops did not hold the position of supremacy which their successors in office have ever since occupied. The progress of this advance can be easily and briefly traced in connection with three great men: Ignatius, (died A.D. 115,) Irenæus, (died A.D. 202,) and Cyprian, (died A.D. 258.)

Ignatius, Bishop of Antioch, is rightly regarded as the great advocate of episcopacy in the earliest age of the church. Although the strength of this view is greatly due to forged epistles that bear his name, his genuine writings warrant it. Now, to him the value of episcopacy is, that it is a *visible centre of unity.* He had in mind the purpose of its origination, which was to avert the danger of disintegration that menaced when Jerusalem had fallen, errors arisen, and apostles were no more. Out of many quotations, a few can be cited. He writes to the Bishop of Smyrna, "Have a care of unity, than which nothing is better." "Let nothing be done without they consent, and do thou nothing without the consent of God." To the people he writes, "Give heed to your bishop, that God also may give heed to you." Such passages show no more than that he valued the office as a security for discipline and harmony in the church, although he may have used language regarding it in which we, in a less ignorant day, could not acquiesce.

The "false Ignatius" who wrote under the great martyr's name, about A.D. 150, goes far beyond all this, and no one has ever made greater claims for episcopal authority. Among other things, he says, "Those live a life after Christ" who "obey the bishop as Jesus Christ." "As many as are of God and of Jesus Christ are with the bishop." "Let no man do any thing pertaining to the church without the bishop." Yet, nevertheless, this unknown writer does not forget the presbyters. They form "a worthy spiritual coronal" around the bishop. They are as the Apostles to Christ, as the council of God. All this was undoubtedly subversive of real Christian liberty, yet we must remember they were troublous times, when one who feared disruptions was not apt to weigh his words; and, furthermore, that obedience, after all, is demanded for the episcopate, not because of any "apostolic succession," or spiritual powers or prerogatives, but because it was the existing government of the church, and obedience was needed for proper harmony and unity.

Irenæus, Bishop of Lyons, wrote his famous work against heretics about seventy years after Ignatius died. In this he expresses his views of the episcopate, and regards it as a depositary of apostolic tradition, a security for the faith. For, amidst the many rival teachers of the day, the perplexed would ask, "What is the test, as to who is right?" Irenæus replies that in the succession of bishops from apostolic days is a means provided for the preservation of the truth, a source of teaching that must be correct. This is a still higher view than that of Ignatius; for the bishops are not only the rulers, to whom unquestioning obedience is to be rendered, but it is furthermore necessary to be in union with them, and to heed them, in order to be sure of possessing the apostolic doctrine, which it was their place to preserve.

Cyprian was Bishop of Carthage from A.D. 248–258, and had a stormy experience. In his writings we find the full-blown flower of episcopal prerogative. He regards the bishop as *the absolute vicegerent of Christ* in things spiritual. He was forced into the episcopate against his will, but he raised it to a position from which it has not yet been deposed. This was due to his great abilities and force of character, as displayed in two contests where he was victor.

The first struggle was in regard to the treatment of those who had, in a recent persecution, yielded and abjured their faith. Confessors (those who had been true in the trial) claimed the right to absolve and restore these "lapsed" brethren, and the clergy of Carthage countenanced these confessors. Cyprian maintained his sole right to this restoration, and fought his whole church. He was sincere, and believed himself doing battle for his Lord and for the welfare of the church. His victory was complete. He triumphed over his clergy, the confessors, and the rival Novatian episcopate, and thus vindicated his supremacy.

The next struggle was with regard to the rebaptism of heretics. Stephen, Bishop of Rome, denied the need thereof, and Cyprian insisted on the rebaptism. The former excommunicated all who practised it. Cyprian convened several synods of bishops, who declared in his favor, and, for the time, he was victorious. The permanent results of the struggle were important, however. It established the independence and the power of the episcopate, and also the principle that the bishops are the absolute representatives of the church. For, while there had been synods before, under Cyprian's guidance they assumed a prominence that had been unknown. He asserted what had not been claimed before, that the office was not a matter of advantage or of rule, or of safety for the truth, but an absolute, incontrovertible establishment by God. He says it is the foundation stone of the ecclesiastical edifice, the primary condition of a church; is appointed by, responsible to, inspired by, God. He defers to the usage of consulting presbyters and laymen, but pleads a direct inspiration, nevertheless, for the office, that enables it to dispense with custom and act alone and independent.

As Cyprian was the great man of his day, and as his victories were so signal in regard to the absolute supremacy of each bishop in his own church, and of the perfect, inspired supremacy of the episcopate in the universal church, these positions were assumed by the other bishops and granted by the church. So was cemented a power that still stands firm, and the structure of episcopal prerogative was complete.

V.

CONCLUSIONS.

We have followed with our author the examination of the government of the church in the New Testament times, and after the close of the Scriptures. We have also examined the relative positions of the bishop and presbyter, and the progress of the rise of the power and sway of the former. From our review, we draw the following inferences:

First, that as far as the Word of God brings us in the history of the church, the form of the ministry was that of the two orders of presbyters and deacons, under the rule of the Apostles. There is no trace of any episcopate save in the apparent prominence of James in the church at Jerusalem.

Second, before the year 100, the state of the times called for a modification in the government of the church, and the episcopate was instituted, probably in imitation of the church at Jerusalem, and, as we can hardly doubt, if this date is correct, with the sanction of St. John. The value of the institution was soon evident, as a bond of union, and it spread from church to church by degrees, until all Christendom, as far as we know, adopted it within a hundred years of the close of the canon of the New Testament.

Third, we have seen that bishops were not intended to be viewed, nor were they viewed, by the church for ages, as successors of the Apostles, holding that position in any sense. The apostles had no successors; their office ceased with them. The episcopate was instituted as a higher rank within the presbytery, and even the great advocates of episcopal prerogative in the early church held this. The idea that they form a *separate order* above the presbyters, equal to that of the Apostles, is a novelty, an invention of man in recent ages.

Fourth, we have seen that, at first, the episcopate had little prerogative, and that was based only upon the duty of obedience to officers; and that the later, and present, elevation was attained by gradual steps, which were not the direction of God nor warranted by the church, even, in any formal way, but which were the result of the seizure of power in troublous times by ambitious men who craved it, and by earnest men, who deemed it necessary for the preservation of the truth and discipline of the church. Episcopacy, as it stood at the end of the third century, and as it stands now, with its power, prestige, and imposing appearance, is the work of man alone, and, as in the different parts of some venerable structure, so here, can we trace the labors of successive builders who added each a portion, until the edifice was entire, from foundation to pinnacle.

Fifth, the quotations and references show us that, even in those early days, and by great and good men, claims on the obedience of the people were advanced, that conflict with Christian liberty and with the equality before God of all believers, as defined in the Scriptures. Hence do we learn that, no matter how eminent they may be, or how close to apostolic times, we dare not follow men as guides. The moment we leave the written Word of God, we are exposed to the perils of human fallibility and human ignorance.

Sixthly. In the Word of God, which is our only authority in matters of faith and of obligation, no permanent form of church government is developed or prescribed. Upon the idea that episcopacy is an essential part of Christianity, man has erected a vast system, with the most uncompromising claims. But it is a pyramid standing on its apex, a structure resting on a point that tapers to nothing. For, as the Bible lays down no form of ecclesiastical polity, none is so morally binding on us that to deviate from it is a sin. No tactual, episcopal, or apostolic succession is hinted at, as a rule, departure from which makes a ministry invalid.

To the episcopal form of church government, properly understood, having its two orders, the diaconate, and the presbyterate with the episcopal preëminence, is to be paid that respect, and it has those claims, which are due and proper in view of its origin and its history. For, it was established by the church, at an early date, in the exercise of a lawful power; it had, at least probably, the sanction of "the beloved disciple;" it saved, under God, the church in the great crisis when it was devised; it has been almost exclusively its government, and that under which it has won great victories; while it binds together, as an historic link, the militant saints of to-day and the triumphant ones of remote ages. The value for us of this form of polity, must, however, be judged by its adaptability to the times with their needs, and by the efficiency it possesses for the great missionary demands of the age, for, not being of divine authority, it is not unchangeable.

But the readjustment of this office is required. It must be brought again into harmony with the rights of the presbytery and of the laity, with the intent of its establishment and with the spirit of scriptural teaching.

The true position of the occupants of the episcopate, as not a superior order of ministers to presbyters, but *primi inter pares*—not absolute rulers, but executive officers—not the depositary of the influences of the Holy Spirit through whom His graces flow to form the church, but a creation of the church wherein the Spirit dwells, and an institution with which the church, that called it into being, can dispense, if deemed necessary—as an accessory, not an essential feature of Christianity—these things must be acknowledged and established, if we are to have a ministry that is fully and truly primitive, and that harmonizes with the nature of the church as "a royal priesthood," having but "one Master, even Christ."

www.ingramcontent.com/pod-product-compliance
Lightning Source LLC
LaVergne TN
LVHW011132110826
845150LV00008B/2297

* 9 7 8 1 4 1 8 1 9 5 0 2 1 *